D1431118

CISTERCIAN STUDIES SERIES: NUMBER NINETY-NINE

ST. BENEDICT'S RULE FOR MONKS

BROTHER PINOCCHIO

ST. BENEDICT'S
RULE FOR MONKS

Br Pinocchio

ST. BENEDICT'S RULE FOR MONKS

SELECTED PASSAGES FROM THE RULE OF ST. BENEDICT
TRANSLATED AND ILLUSTRATED BY BR. PINOCCHIO,
A CISTERCIAN AT
OUR LADY OF SPRINGBANK ABBEY
SPARTA WISCONSIN

CISTERCIAN PUBLICATIONS INC.
Kalamazoo, Michigan

Excerpts from the *Regula monachorum sancti Benedicti*,
translated by the illustrator.

Available in Britain and Europe from
A. R. Mowbray & Co Ltd
St Thomas House   Becket Street
Oxford OX1 1SJ

Available elsewhere (including Canada) from
Cistercian Publications Inc
WMU Station
Kalamazoo, Michigan 49008

*The work of Cistercian Publications is made possible in part by support
from Western Michigan University to the Institute of Cistercian Studies.*

Library of Congress Cataloguing in Publication Data:

Benedict, Saint, Abbot of Monte Cassino.
  St. Benedict's rule for monks.

  (Cistercian studies series ; 99)
  1. Benedictines—Rules.   2. Monasticism and religious
orders—Rules.   I. Pinocchio, Brother.   II. Title.
III. Series.
BX3004.E6   1987   255'.106   86-24465
ISBN 0-87907-899-5
ISBN 0-87907-999-1 (pbk.)

Book design by Alice M. Duthie

TO ABBOT JOSEPH VAN GREVENBROEK, O'CIST WHO RECEIVED ME INTO HIS FAMILY AS A FATHER RECEIVES A SON. TO YOU, FATHER, I OWE MY FIRST ENCOUNTERS WITH ST. BENEDICT'S "LOVING FATHER".

PREFACE

THIS SMALL WORK GREW FROM A FEW DRAWINGS PRESENTED TO DOM JOSEPH VAN GREVENBROEK, SECOND ABBOT OF OUR LADY OF SPRING BANK, ON THE OCCASION OF THE TENTH ANNIVERSARY OF HIS ABBATIAL ELECTION. IT WAS LATER SUGGESTED THAT I EXPAND THE NUMBER OF DRAWINGS, TRANSLATE THE ORIGINAL LATIN INTO ENGLISH AND THEN PUBLISH THIS SMALL COLLECTION. IT HAS TAKEN SEVERAL YEARS OF INTERRUPTED WORK, BEFORE ST. BENEDICT'S RULE FOR MONKS REACHED ITS PRESENT FORM.

BEFORE CONTINU-ING FURTHER, I
SHOULD LIKE TO APOLO-GIZE TO ALL
ARTISTS, LATINISTS, AND ENGLISH SCHOLARS
FOR MY SOMEWHAT ROUGH AND UN-
REFINED WISCONSIN STYLE. I FIND MY
GREATEST "SINS" HAVE BEEN
COMMITTED AS TRANSLATOR,
BUT I SHIELD MYSELF BEHIND
THE ADAGE: TRANSLATOR,
TRAITOR." FOR THOSE
SEEKING A TIGHTLY
LITERAL, OR WELL POLISHED
ENGLISH TRANSLATION;
I APOLOGIZE, FOR NEITHER
OF THESE WERE MY GOAL,
I DESIRED TO TRANSLATE THE
RULE INTO AN ENGLISH THAT
IS NOT TOO ARTIFICIAL, BUT
SIMPLE & DIRECT AS THE
DRAW- INGS THEMSELVES.

AVE ARIA

NOT ONLY THE DRAWINGS HAVE
PLAYED A ROLE IN MY TRANSLATION, BUT
ALSO MY SUBJECTIVE IMPRESSIONS
NURTURED BY TWO PHRASES FROM
THE PROLOGUE OF THE RULE.
SINCE MY ENTRANCE INTO THE
MONASTERY, I HAVE ALWAYS ENJOYED
THE PRESENCE OF ST. BENEDICT'S
"LOVING FATHER" IN MY OWN
FATHER ABBOT, IN OUR FATHER IMMED-
IATE, IN THE ABBOT PRESIDENT OF
OUR CONGREGATION AND IN OUR ABBOT
GENERAL. I HAVE WITNESSED THE
LOVE AND CARE OF FATHERS FOR
THEIR CHILDREN THROUGH THESE
MEN I SEE THAT THE LOVING
FATHER AT SUBIACO AND MONTE
CASINO, HAS THRIVED AND
IS ALIVE WITHIN OUR CISTERCIAN
ORDER. THUS ONE OF MY INTENTIONS IN THIS
WORK IS TO THANK THEM FOR BRINGING THIS
ASPECT OF ST. BENEDICT TO LIFE.

THE SECOND OF THE TWO INFLUENTIAL PHRASES DOES NOT APPEAR IN THIS PRESENT WORK, BUT I STILL HOLD IT TO BE IMPORTANT IN ORDER TO UNDERSTAND ST. BENEDICT'S INTENTIONS IN CERTAIN PRESCRIPTIONS OF THE RULE. "IN ESTABLISHING THIS SCHOOL OF THE LORD'S SERVICE, WE HOPE WE SHALL SET DOWN NOTHING HARSH NOR BURDENSOME." THUS, CERTAIN SUPERLATIVES, WHICH IN ST. BENEDICT'S TIME SEEMED CALM, BUT MAY CAUSE MODERN MAN TO SHUDDER, HAVE BEEN TONED DOWN OR RESTATED IN A MORE AGREEABLE FASHION, IN ORDER TO QUELL THE FEARS OF CERTAIN SENSITIVITIES.

I DESIRE TO COMMUNICATE AND SHARE WITH YOU THE LOVE, JOY, PEACE AND LIBERTY THAT I HAVE FOUND IN MY CISTERCIAN VOCATION, AND THROUGH THIS SMALL WORK, RESTATE ST. BENEDICT'S INVITATION:

"WHOSOEVER YOU ARE, HURRYING TO YOUR HEAVENLY HOMELAND WITH THE HELP OF CHRIST, LIVE THIS LITTLE RULE WRITTEN FOR BEGINNERS. THEN, UNDER GOD'S PROTECTION, YOU SHALL ARRIVE AT THE VERY HEIGHTS OF WISDOM & VIRTUE, AMEN."

BR. PINOCCHIO

INRI

THE ABB-
BELIEVED
CHRIST.
MONASTERY.

OT IS.
TO ACT AS
IN THE
CHAPTER 2

BR PINOCCHIO

WHENEVER ANY MATTER OF IMPORTANCE IS TO BE SETTLED IN THE MONASTERY, LET THE ABBOT CALL THE ENTIRE COMMUNITY TOGETHER & PUT FORTH THE MATTER UNDER QUESTION. AFTER HAVING HEARD THE BROTHERS' ADVICE, LET HIM REFLECT AND THEN FOLLOW WHATEVER COURSE HE BELIEVES TO BE THE BEST.

CHAPTER 3

BR PINUCCHIO

THE FIRST STEP OF HUMILITY IS OBEDIENCE WITHOUT DELAY, WHICH COMES NATURALLY TO THOSE WHO CHERISH NOTHING MORE THAN CHRIST.... ACCOMPLISHING THE SUPERIOR'S COMMAND AS PROMPTLY AS IF IT HAD COME FROM GOD HIMSELF. CHAPTER 5

BR. PINOCCHIO

THE FIFTH DEGREE OF HUMILITY IS SHOWN WHEN THE MONK CONFESSES TO HIS ABBOT, IN ALL HUMILITY, ALL THE EVIL THOUGHTS HE MAY SHELTER IN HIS HEART, OR THE SINS HE HAS COMMITTED IN SECRET, RATHER THAN HIDE THEM.

CHAPTER 7

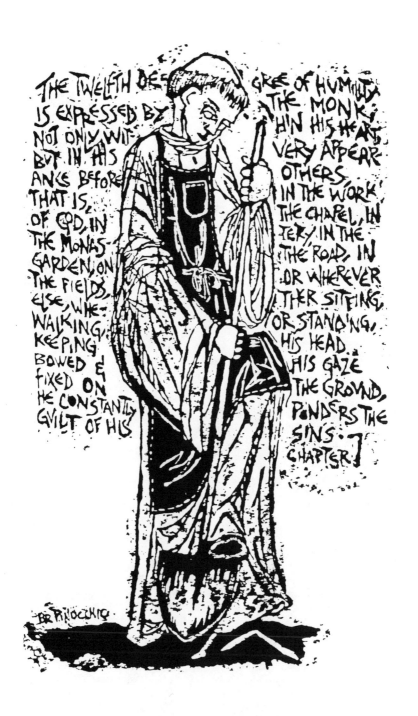

THE TWELFTH DEGREE OF HUMILITY IS EXPRESSED BY THE MONK NOT ONLY WITH HIS HEART BUT IN HIS VERY APPEARANCE BEFORE OTHERS THAT IS, IN THE WORK OF GOD, IN THE CHAPEL, IN THE MONAS TERY, IN THE GARDEN, ON THE ROAD, IN THE FIELDS OR WHEREVER ELSE, WHETHER SITTING, WALKING, OR STANDING, KEEPING HIS HEAD BOWED & HIS GAZE FIXED ON THE GROUND, HE CONSTANTLY PONDERS THE GUILT OF HIS SINS. CHAPTER 7

BR PINOCHIO

LET THE OFFICES OF LAUDS AND VESPERS NEVER TERMINATE WITH-OUT THE SUPERIOR'S RECITING THE LORD'S PRAYER, WHILE ALL LISTEN, ON ACCOUNT OF THE THORNS OF SCANDAL WHICH TEND TO CROP UP. BEING WARNED BY THE COMMITMENT THEY MAKE IN THE WORDS "FORGIVE US AS WE FORGIVE", THEY WILL CHASE THIS VICE FROM THEIR MIDST.

PINOCCHIO

CHAPTER 13

FROM THE EASTER-COST LET SUNG WITH HOLY FEAST OF UNTIL PENTE- ALELUIA BE THE PSALMS AND RESPON- SORIES WITHOUT INTERRUPTION. CHAPTER 15:

C BR PINOCCHIO

THE PSALTER WITH ITS FULL HUNDRED & FIFTY PSALMS SHOULD BE CHANTED EVERY WEEK, BEING BEGUN ANEW AT VIGILS ON SUNDAY, FOR THOSE MONKS WHO, DURING ONE WEEK, SING LESS THAN THE PSALTER WITH ITS CUSTOMARY CANTICLES SHOW THEM SELVES TO BE LAZY IN THEIR SERVICE OF DEVOTION.

BR. PINOCCHIO

CHAPTER 19

WE OUGHT TO PRESENT OUR SUPPLICATIONS TO THE LORD, GOD OF THE UTMOST HUM-PURITY OF ALL WITH ILITY AND DEVOTION. AND LET US KNOW THAT IT IS NOT IN THE MULTIPLICATION OF OUR WORDS THAT HEAR US, BUT IN OF HEART AND TEARS OF COMPUNCTION.

GOD WILL OUR PURITY

CHAPTER 20

BR. PINOCCHIO

WHEN THEY ARISE TO PERFORM THE WORK OF GOD, LET THE BROTHERS GENTLY ENCOURAGE ONE ANOTHER, FOR THE SLEEPY ARE PRONE TO MAKE EXCUSES.

CHAPTER 22

LET THE PUNISHMENTS
OF EXCOMMUNICATION
OR OTHER DISCIPLINARY
MEASURES FIT THE
CRIME, THE SERIOUSNESS OF WHICH
THE ABBOT SHALL BE THE JUDGE.
A BROTHER FOUND GUILTY OF A LESS
SERIOUS FAULT SHALL BE DEPRIVED
OF SHARING THE COMMON TABLE.

BR. PINOCHIO   CHAPTER 24

THE ABBOT MUST SHOW THE GREATEST CONCERN FOR THE FALLEN BROTHERS, FOR IT IS NOT THE HEALTHY WHO NEED A DOCTOR, BUT THOSE WHO ARE ILL. AND SO, LET HIM USE EVERY POSSIBLE REMEDY AS A GOOD DOCTOR

CHAPTER 27

IF A BROTHER, WHO
HAS LEFT THE MONASTERY
BY HIS OWN FAULT SHOULD
WISH TO RETURN,
LET HIM BE RECIEVED
BACK, THOUGH
IN THE LOWEST
PLACE. CHAPTER 29

AS CELLARER OF THE MONASTERY, LET A MAN BE CHOSEN FROM THE COMMUNITY, WHO IS WISE, OF MATURE CONDUCT, TEMPERATE, NOT ONE WHO OVEREATS, NOR IS PROUD, EXCITABLE, OFFENSIVE, SLUGGISH, OR WASTEFUL, BUT WHO IS GOD-FEARING, & LIKE A FATHER TO THE ENTIRE COMMUNITY.

CHAPTER 31

BR. PINOCCHIO.

ABOVE ALL & BEFORE ALL THINGS, LET THE GREATEST CARE BE TAKEN OF THE SICK, THAT THEY MAY BE TREATED AS CHRIST, FOR HE SAID: "I WAS SICK AND YOU VISITED ME"

CHAPTER 36

BR FINOCCHIO

LET READING ALWAYS ACCOMPANY THE MEALS OF THE BROTHERS,... THERE SHOULD BE COMPLETE SILENCE, NO WHISPERING, NO SPEAKING, BUT ONLY THE SOUND OF THE VOICE OF THE READER. CHAPTER 38

BR PINOCCIO

AT THE SOUND OF THE BELL CALLING THEM TO PRAYER, LET THE BROTHERS DROP WHATEVER THEY HAVE IN HAND, AND GO QUICKLY, YET WITH GRAVITY, SO AS NOT TO GIVE RISE TO CLOWNING.

AND, SO, NOTHING SHALL BE GIVEN PRECEDENCE TO THE WORK OF GOD.

CHAPTER 43

BR PINOCCHIO

HE WHO HAS BEEN EXCOMMUN-
ICATED, UPON BEING RE-INTRO-
DUCED AMONG THE
BROTHERS IN
CHOIR, WILL
HUMBLE
HIMSELF
BEFORE THE
ABBOT &
THEN
BEFORE
THE OTHERS
ASKING
THEM
TO
PRAY
FOR
HIM.

CHAPTER 44

BR PINOCCHIO

IF ANYONE SHOULD COMMIT A FAULT WHILE AT WORK, WHETHER HE BE IN THE KITCHEN, THE CELLAR, OR SERVING, WHETHER WORKING IN THE BAKEHOUSE, IN THE GARDEN, OR IN ANY WORK-SHOP WHATEVER, BY BREAK-ING OR LOSING SOMETHING, OR BY FAILING IN ANY OTHER MANNER ANY-WHERE, LET HIM COME IMMEDIATELY AND ADMIT HIS FAULT BEFORE THE ABBOT & THE COMMUNITY.

CHAPTER 46

BR. PPINOCCHIO

THE NOU- FOR

CHARGE OF AN-
NCING THE HOURS
THE WORK OF GOD,
BOTH DAY AND
NIGHT IS CON-
FIDED TO
THE ABBOT
HE MAY DO IT
HIMSELF, OR MAY
GATE THE RESPONSIB-
TO A CAREFUL BROTHER
THAT EVERYTHING
BE DONE AT ITS
PER TIME.
CHAPTER 47

DELE-
UITY
SO
MAY
PRO-

BR. PINOCCHIO.

IF THE NEEDS OR THE POVERTY
OF THE PLACE DEMAND
THAT THE BROTHERS
GATHER IN THE HARVEST,
LET THEM NOT BE
DISHEARTENED, FOR
THEY ARE TRULY MONKS
WHEN THEY LIVE
FROM THE WORK OF
THEIR HANDS.
CHAPTER 48

BROTHERS WHO WORK FAR FROM THE MONASTERY AND CAN NOT ARRIVE TO THE CHAPEL AT THE APP- ONTED TIMES FOR THE ROV- ERS, SHOULD REC- ITE THE OFFICE WHERE THEY ARE WORKING WITH THE ABBOT'S APPROVAL.

CHAPTER 50

IF A BRO-
WISH TO GO
TO PRAY PRI-
SIMPLY GO
NOT IN
A LOW
VOI-
CE
BUT
&
FER-

THER SHOULD
TO THE CHAPEL
JATELY, LET HIM
IN AND PRAY:

IN TEARS
IN HEARTFELT
VOR: 52
CHAPTER

BR. PINOCCHIO

UNDER ORDINARY CONDI-
TIONS, WE BELIEVE THAT
THE FOLLOWING CLO-
THING SHOULD
BE ENOUGH FOR
EACH MONK:
A COWL, A
TUNIC...&
A SCAPULAR
WORN AT WORK
AND FOR
THEIR FEET,
BOOTS AND
SHOES.
CHAPTER 55

BR. PINOCCHIO

IF THERE ARE
CRAFTSMEN IN THE
MONASTERY, LET
THEM HUMBLY
CARRY ON THEIR
CRAFTS.
CHAPTER 57

IF A PILGRIM MONK
SHOULD ARRIVE FROM
AFAR, ASKING HOS-
PITALITY, LET HIM BE
RECEIVED FOR AS
LONG AS HE
WISHES, PROVIDED
THAT HE CONTENTS
HIMSELF WITH THE
LIFE AS IT IS.
CHAPTER 61

LET NOT HIS PRIESTHOOD BE A REASON FOR HIM TO FORGET THE OBEDIENCE AND THE DISCIPLINE OF THE RULE,

BUT MAY HE ALWAYS GROW CLOSER AND CLOSER TO GOD.

CHAPTER 62

BR PINOCCHIO

LET A WISE ELDERLY BROTHER TAKE CARE OF THE DOOR OF THE MONASTERY.

CHAPTER 66

BR PINOCCHIO

WHOSOEVER YOU ARE, HURRYING TO YOUR HEAVENLY HOMELAND, WITH THE HELP OF CHRIST, LIVE THIS LITTLE RULE FOR BEGINNERS, SO THAT UNDER GOD'S PROTECTION YOU MAY IN THE END REACH THE VERY HEIGHTS OF WISDOM & VIRTUE. AMEN.

Holy Rule

PINOCCHIO   CHAPTER 73

ACKNOWLEDGEMENTS

THANKS ARE DUE TO SEVERAL PEOPLE FOR
THE REALIZATION OF THIS BOOK:
FIRST, TO FR. BLAISE FUEZ, OUR PRIOR,
WHOSE INITIAL EFFORTS BROUGHT THIS WORK
TO THE ROAD OF PUBLICATION
SECONDLY, TO FRA. JEOFFREY SEAGRAVES,
WHOSE CORRECTIONS AND COMMENTS WERE
WELL APPECIATED.

CISTERCIAN PUBLICATIONS INC.

Kalamazoo, Michigan

TITLES LISTING

THE CISTERCIAN FATHERS SERIES

Texts and Studies
in the
Monastic Tradition

THE CISTERCIAN STUDIES SERIES

MONASTIC TEXTS

CHRISTIAN SPIRITUALITY

MONASTIC STUDIES

CISTERCIAN STUDIES

Medieval Religious Women

Temporarily out of print   † Forthcoming

---

* *Temporarily out of print*   † *Forthcoming*